poems / fragments

STILL AT LARGE

poems / fragments

FRANK STEWART

EL LÉON LITERARY ARTS

BERKELEY

For my brother,

CES

1954–2020

Cover illustration: Marc Chagall, *Over the Town/Over Vitebsk*, 1918. Oil on Canvas, 141x197 cm. Tretyakov Gallery, Moscow, Russia.

Text illustrations: Marc Chagall etchings and lithographs are used with permission, courtesy of the National Gallery of Art, Museum of Modern Art, and Artists Rights Society (ARS), New York / ADAGP, Paris. See page 69 for complete illustration credits.

The poems "Goats" and "Conviction," first appeared in slightly different form in *Poet Lore* 112 (Spring/Summer) 2017.

Still at Large is published by
El León Literary Arts
Berkeley, California
elleonliteraryarts.org

Distributed by Small Press Distributors, Inc.
1341 Seventh Street
Berkeley, California 94710
www.spdbooks.org

ISBN 978-0-9891277-9-0
DESIGNED AND PRODUCED BY BARBARA POPE BOOK DESIGN
PRINTED IN CHINA

One should be thankful, nowadays,
each day the sun shines
and one is still at large.

ETTY HILLESUM, THE NETHERLANDS, 1942

*

In order for your own voice to be heard again,
nearer and more vividly,
I link your language to mine from time to time,
inserting in quotes some of the phrases
taken from your writings.
May these portions of your posthumous message,
brought together and presented by me,
serve to open the heart and the mind
of the one who reads them!

EMANUELE ARTOM, TURIN, ITALY, DECEMBER 20, 1940

*

It's good to know everything.

SHMUEL ROTEM CZERNIAKÓW, POLAND, 1930S

CONTENTS

Preface xi

Prologue xiii

PART ONE

Conviction 1

Night 2

I Tell You 3

Mother 4

Wake Up 5

The Feast of Vandavar 6

At the Train Station 7

That's Why 8

The Open Field 8

They Went to the City Hall 9

The Book 10

Cucumbers 11

Turkish Harem 12

Also 13

Who Knew? 14

Beauty, the Oldest Sorrow 15

Deportees 16

The Afterlife 17

Who Would? 18

Pigs 19

Friendship 20
And Forever 21

PART TWO

Like God 23
Beautiful 24
His Eyes 25
Father 26
Today 27
Mother 28
So 29
Who Do We Thank? 30
Bridge of Ravens 31
Obviously 32
Sunday Morning 33
Sooner or Later 34
A Journey 35
Hardly Any 36
A Thin Ray of Brightness 37
More Light 38
One Night 39
Escape 40

Goats 41
Off the Coast, a Ship 42
Abandoned 43
Coral Island Rain 44
The Finest Thing 45
Defiance 46
The Sunflower 47

PART THREE

Pancakes 49
Foreigners 50
Dear Diary 51
Precisely 52
On the Buses 53
Music 54
I Told Them 55
Look, Look 56
The Plan 57

For the Record 58
OK 58
Bit by Bit 59
Exile 60
Be 61
Sugar 62
What Else? 63
Just So 64
Graffiti 65
Decency 66

Epilogue 67
Marc Chagall Illustrations 69
Sources 71
Selected Readings 77
About the Author 82

PREFACE

In his notebooks in 1941, Camus wrote, "Everything is decided. It is simple and straightforward. But then human suffering intervenes and alters all our plans." The majority of poems and fragments here are moments when plans and suffering intersect in the lives of ordinary men and women—that is, people whose lives are seen as small, traceless, and insignificant. Of course, all lives are significant and consequential to the person who experiences them, and they become so to the rest of us when we recognize that each human life is small but also miraculous in the face of evil.

The poems/fragments are arranged, with few exceptions, chronologically, as an historical context may be helpful to understand the feelings and experiences expressed in them. However, they could be read in any order and have the same coherence and effect. History is simply a collection of moments, like the ones represented here, which are given meaning when fleeting, insignificant lives are held up to the light. The light is at the bottom of the sea of moments we swim in, and all that's required to make that light illuminate them is a few words in a solitary, recognizably human voice.

A few of the pieces here are nearly verbatim from the sources where I found them; all sources are noted at the back. Each poem/fragment has been shaped and sharpened by me in some way, but certainly none of them is wholly mine. The experiences of the people in them are not mine, either. I link them together here in the hope they will "open the heart and the mind of the one who reads them."

PROLOGUE

FOR NOW

What is that which we hang onto
And which is snuffed out in a second?

I have not yet found a poem that
Encompasses what is happening here—

Much must remain forever unsaid,
Saved up for the hour when

It is handed down to people,
Without mediation.

THE RUSSIAN FRONT, MAY–JUNE 1940

Marc Chagall

PART ONE

CONVICTION

They asked if the bird was dead
—because they were all starving

then a boy picked it up
and carefully rearranged its wings

any of us could have said no
the boy clutched the bird tighter

then a creaking saddle
caused them to look behind

so no one saw what happened next
the rider seemed to them wonderful at first
and took their breath away

KARS, RUSSIAN EMPIRE, 1912

NIGHT

Then they walked for 5 or 6 hours
until they reached a place called Valanidia.

Some slept in the carts, while others lay on the ground.
During the night the Turks came. They wanted to take all the girls.

But the policemen escorting them resisted,
as well as the others, young and old,
and they didn't take them and no one slept.

AYVALIK, OTTOMAN EMPIRE, 1914

I TELL YOU

The Turks conscripted my father
And this saved us from being rounded up.

You see, the governor in Homs
Sent the village prefect an order

To "poison all the dogs," which meant
Us Armenians. But the prefect,
Djemal Pasha, knew us.

He ordered the police
To kill all the stray dogs in the streets.

So we were saved. Then he ordered
All the Armenians to change their names.

HOMS, OTTOMAN EMPIRE, 1914

MOTHER

That night there was nowhere to sleep
Mother slept on the ground
My sister, Khatoun, and me
Sitting near mother
Braiding her hair. A woman passing
Looked at us and said
"Why, the poor darlings,
They don't know their mother has died."
We were children, how could we know that?

HOMS, OTTOMAN EMPIRE, 1914

WAKE UP

You don't seem to understand what we want.
We want an Armenia without Armenians.

ANKARA, OTTOMAN EMPIRE, DECEMBER 1915

THE FEAST OF VARDAVAR

After the Turks lit the church
Packed with villagers
Intoxicated and merry soldiers danced
Swinging their sabers, beating their chests
They sang
yürü yavrum, yürü!
Dance, children, dance!
I wish my eyes had become blind
So that I would not see
We escaped but I swear
To me they looked like wild beasts

OTTOMAN EMPIRE, 1915

AT THE TRAIN STATION

At the train station, we saw them pleading,
"No! Wait! We will become Muslims! We
will become Germans! We will become
anything you want!" Then the train took them
to Kemah Pass where they cut their throats.

OUTSIDE ERZINCAN, OTTOMAN EMPIRE, 1915

THAT'S WHY

When we could get flour
Our father would knead it
And boil the grass, chop it,
And salt and pepper the flour
And we would eat it. When
You are hungry, grass is
Better than honey or steak

OTTOMAN EMPIRE, 1915

AN OPEN FIELD

Farther from the town we reached
An open field. We saw all
The animals had been gathered there,

Our sheep, cows, horses, and so on.
My aunt jumped over the fence
And went over to our cows, hugging them.

But there were soldiers on both sides of
The road to make sure no one swerved
And everyone kept up.

OTTOMAN EMPIRE, 1915

THEY WENT TO THE CITY HALL

And a judge told him, "Child,
Your religion is very bad
And must be renounced. Do you
Renounce it?" He said, *evet, effendi,*
Yes, sir. "Do you accept the real religion,
The Muslim religion?" *Evet, effendi.*
The judge said, "Son, your name henceforth
Will be Abdul Rahman oghlu Assad.

Then they gave the boy a fez
And a turban so everyone would know
He was Muslim. Then he had to be
Circumcised, so a religious leader did that.
Afterwards, he could safely go out
On the street. But even then
The Turkish boys would taunt him,
Calling him *dönme,* turncoat.

OTTOMAN EMPIRE, 1915

THE BOOK

I had a leather water bottle
Containing about a cup full of water
The children near me were crying
Choor! Choor! Water! Water!
Without being seen
I held out the bottle quickly
Here and there to moisten
The children's lips with a few drops
I think those drops
Were very precious, and that they were
Recorded in the book of heaven

BETWEEN MARASH AND DIER EL-ZOR,
OTTOMAN EMPIRE, JUNE 1915

CUCUMBERS

After two hours of walking from Marash
We were near a resting place
The Turkish guards were doing their latest gleaning
They scattered among the convoy
Taking whatever they wanted to take—
A hat, a shoe, a gown, a belt, a watch
They took and they took

Nearby there was a cucumber garden
Those who had any money left
Bought some cucumbers and began
To eat them ravenously
I wanted a cucumber too
But I did not have the money to buy one
I began to sob like a child

BETWEEN MARASH AND DIER EL-ZOR,
OTTOMAN EMPIRE, JUNE 1915

TURKISH HAREM

They wore long, blue, sleeveless caftans
And scarves over their shoulders
To shield their faces against the desert winds
Some covered their heads with turbans

Some had cushions on their heads
Which protected them as they carried heavy loads
Some had babies in cloth bags on their backs
Some displayed rings in their nostrils

And had garish, dark-blue tattoos
On their faces, bosoms, hands, arms, ankles,
And even their kneecaps
These women were the lucky ones

RAS AL-AYN DESERT, OTTOMAN EMPIRE, 1915

ALSO

Even the Kurds were appalled.

VAN, OTTOMAN EMPIRE, 1915

WHO KNEW?

Remembering
the advice of the young woman
in Ras al-Zor

Mama had hidden
three lira
in her rectum

But we dared not use them
to buy food. We knew
the guards would take them
if they knew

RAS AL-AYN DESERT,
OTTOMAN EMPIRE, 1915

BEAUTY, THE OLDEST SORROW

By blackening their faces with dirt or soot
Many girls tried to make themselves ugly
Mama would caution me everyday

"Vergeen, don't forget to rub dirt on your face"
She was afraid a soldier would take notice
Of me, I was thirteen

RAS AL-AYN DESERT, OTTOMAN EMPIRE, 1915

DEPORTEES

In the depths of the cedar forest
They came upon tents of black goatskins,
The shelters of Turkish charcoal makers.

"We would have been so happy,"
The priest wrote, "to remain in that solitude,
To live simply and free from
The unbearable eyes of the guards.

"We envied those poor workers
But also the startled rabbits that
Jumped from beneath bushes and
Dashed away. And we envied birds
Free to fly wherever they wished.

"But we were going to the desert
To become handfuls of dust."

TAURUS MOUNTAINS, OTTOMAN EMPIRE, 1916

THE AFTERLIFE

During the deportation
I spoke to the captain. "Bey," I said,
"As a priest, I frighten my congregation
When I tell them their sins
Will make them suffer in the next world
If they don't atone.
How will you atone for yours?"

"I already atone for mine," he said.
"After each massacre
I spread my prayer rug and say my namaz,
Thanking Allah
For making me worthy for this jihad.

"My friends wanted me to retire
On account of my old age.
It's a good thing I didn't."

LEAVING YOZGAT, OTTOMAN EMPIRE, 1916

WHO WOULD?

Finally we got to Mardin
where there were trains for Aleppo.
We had lost our human appearance:
our hair was long, and our clothes
were not normal clothes.
The nurses in white uniforms asked us
if we wanted to go to America.
My mother said no.

MARDIN, OTTOMAN EMPIRE, 1918

PIGS

In the assembly, Mazhar Mufit shouted
If a pig swallowed a diamond,
Should you spare the diamond or spare the pig?
Do not sacrifice the gem
By sparing the Armenian swine!

ANKARA, OTTOMAN EMPIRE, 1920

FRIENDSHIP

After the French soldiers withdrew from Marash
We who had hidden were weak with hunger.
The town was full of Turks firing their weapons.
Only Peter, my American friend living there,
Would go with me to the Turkish grain shop
to barter for food. A Turk suddenly ran toward us
And embraced him. "My friend!" he exclaimed,
"How fortunate you did not come to me
For protection! I would have had to kill you."

MARASH, TURKEY, 16 FEBRUARY 1920

AND FOREVER

We had to walk bent over
To avoid hitting the low beams
That hold up the trench.
And it was very cold. The mud

Was like chewing gum. We slipped
On the duckboards. A mortar shell
Exploded in the trees nearby.

She was there to write about it.
She was impressed by how calm
The young soldiers were.
"You seem at home here," she said to one.

"The trenches are good," he told her.
"We've been here a long time."
Machine guns echoed from
Across the Puente de los Franceses.
"If necessary," the boy said,
"We can stay here forever."

MADRID, SPAIN, NOVEMBER 1937

PART TWO

LIKE GODS

First pork leg, then roast calf,
Sausage with vegetables, and
To finish a wonderful dessert,
Apricots with cherries,

And then to go with it, two bottles of red
Wine. And the whole meal cost
Only nine francs!

That's seventy-five German pfennig.
Yes, yes, you're right. We're living
Like gods in France.

TOULON, FRANCE, JUNE 1940

BEAUTIFUL

The way they acted was so proper, so magnificent, so disciplined; they command nothing but respect. The locals could learn a lot from them. Just look at them marching by, on foot or on horseback or with their guns, looking so beautiful, so healthy, and with such cheerful faces; they're big and sturdy and very neat, making you reflect, inadvertently, on what a pitiful army we have! Our people here are so rude and impolite, while they are so proper! It's easy to see the difference. How dare we fight such a powerful, strong people? No wonder we had to give up after four days, the difference was too great.

THE HAGUE, THE NETHERLANDS, 1940

HIS EYES

A policeman came to their apartment
And wanted to take some of their things.

The woman cried, pleading that
she was a widow with a child.

He said he would take nothing
If she could guess correctly

which of his eyes was the artificial one.
When she guessed the left

he asked her how she knew. Because,
she said, that one has a human look.

WARSAW, POLAND, 8 NOVEMBER 1940

FATHER

I was the girl who played soccer with the boys.
I was the girl who rode a bicycle on the street
Which a lot of Jewish girls didn't do that.

See, I was born a fighter. I am free. I was always free.
When I was a child my father used to say
That I am dangerous.

LOKOV, POLAND, 1940

TODAY

Today it's so cold
You can pass by the guards at the gate
Without having to take your hat off.

WARSAW, POLAND, 31 DECEMBER 1940

MOTHER

The night was our mother.

FORESTS OF LITHUANIA, 1941

SO

It was all very quick.
We were ordered to watch

And then we went back inside, as if
Nothing had happened

THE RUSSIAN FRONT, 1941

WHO DO WE THANK?

Now, you can celebrate:
a leper is given bread,
everyone gets a fair death-price.

Tell them I am 13 today,
red hair, pink nails,
I am sure my mother and sister are alive.

CHIOS, GREECE, 1941

BRIDGE OF RAVENS

The new women were holding onto their small bundles
They'd been allowed to take with them—
Curtains, a pot of lard, black bread, a coat.
To them we looked like striped silhouettes without faces.
They didn't know why this was happening to them
Or why they were here. They knew nothing.
At least we knew why we were here.

RAVENSBRÜCK, GERMANY, 1942

OBVIOUSLY

Obviously it is
Inconvenient

To shoot everybody,
He explained.

KIEV, USSR, APRIL 1942

SUNDAY MORNING

"The umpteenth year of the war..."
Are you happy now?

AMSTERDAM, THE NETHERLANDS, 1942

SOONER OR LATER

The wind squealed under the floor
The train had stopped
Outside you could see a skinny horse beside a wire fence
This time no one got off
To look for the missing children

CENTRAL EUROPE, 1943

A JOURNEY

From the train we moved five in a row
I was weak and someone put out a hand
I thought it was to help me, but
It was to hit me
"Russian pigs! Russian bandits!"

Nobody could understand
Why they were being beaten
We hadn't learned yet
That this was just the way they behaved

RAVENSBRÜCK, GERMANY, 1943

HARDLY ANY

Hardly any prisoners were taken
And the few we held
Would thrash about and bite.

METZ, GERMANY, 9 SEPTEMBER 1944

A THIN RAY OF BRIGHTNESS

Before dawn, it was hard to see the roads.
We had to concentrate to avoid driving
into the ditches.
At the top of a hill
we could see the outlines of Luxembourg.
The road cut through a forest onto the plain.
The taillights of the tank ahead
Guided us through the darkness.
The most beautiful thing I had ever seen.

OUTSIDE LUXEMBOURG, BELGIUM, 1944

MORE LIGHT

Outside we saw ragged women pillaging,
Their shoulder blades thin as knives.

Some stumbled into the river,
Others twisted their skirts up to defecate.

We didn't see no infants except
A red-haired girl with inflamed skin

Who looked like she was sleeping.
Villagers brought us hot broth and horsemeat.

Later, three of us got down from the train
To see if anyone was around

The only light we had was some stolen candles
Which weren't enough.

CENTRAL EUROPE, 1944

ONE NIGHT

In the silence I heard
From the ruins
Someone playing Chopin's
"Etiuda Rewolucyjna."
Now can you hear it?

WARSAW, POLAND, 1944

ESCAPE

The smoke was stifling
And people tripped in the darkness.

WOLA SUBURB, WARSAW, POLAND,
AUGUST 1944

GOATS

Old women dragged sleds
Overloaded with kids and moldy bedding
Men was staggering
Under the worthless furniture they carried
Many fell exhausted onto their knees
At dusk, with no place to bathe or shit
A lot lay in the ditches to sleep
The refugees smelled like goats
We all did
The coal-black snow was lighted by the moon—
Muddy footprints leading from a shallow river
Was turning to ice

CENTRAL EUROPE, 1945

OFF THE COAST, A SHIP

Agitating the heavy water,
Drunk on goblets of black crude,
A shark thrashes out to sea.

SOUTHERN OKINAWA, 1945

ABANDONED

The sweet May rain
Runs down my cheeks.

In a rice paddy
An unexploded artillery shell
Wallows in the mud.

SOUTHERN OKINAWA, 1945

CORAL ISLAND RAIN

The horn blares twice,
The bus halts in the neon rain.
The red fins of her raincoat fluttering,
The woman swims off the bus, into
The streetlight's shadow.

SOUTHERN OKINAWA, 1945

THE FINEST THING

You must be attached body and soul
And with all the forces of your heart
And character to him.

You must regard yourself as his children
Whom nothing on earth
Could ever make waver
From unconditional loyalty.

This is the greatest and finest thing
In a man's life—unconditional and
Loyal devotion to the great man
Who is your leader.

RADIO BROADCAST, BERLIN, GERMANY, 20 FEBRUARY 1945

DEFIANCE

He was defiant at his trial
When the judge asked him
How he'd been able to betray

His fellow partisans, he replied
"For a million bucks
You would have done the same thing"

PRAGUE, CZECHOSLOVAKIA, 1945

THE SUNFLOWER

I knew there was little I could say to this mother...
She would prefer to think me a slanderer
Than acknowledge her son's crime...

She kept repeating the words, "He was such a good boy,"
As if she wished me to confirm it.
But that I could not do.

In his boyhood he had certainly been
A "good boy." But a graceless period of his life
Had turned him into a murderer.

STUTTGART, GERMANY, 1946

Marc Chagall

PART THREE

PANCAKES

They began wandering in circles
Because of the darkness and heavy snow.
Luminescent flares streaked through the heavens.

One of them said he swore he could see
His mother bringing warm pancakes
For everyone. Those who did not die of the cold

Were captured by the Chetniks because
Their feet were frozen, or because
A child would begin crying.

BIRAĆ MOUNTAINS, 1992

FOREIGNERS

The children asked their teacher,
Who was from Algeria, why after
All her years living in Paris

She walked down the street zigzag.
"This is how you avoid a bullet,"
She answered. How strange they all

Had thought—until much later
When they returned to Croatia
And the bombing began.

ZAGREB, CROATIA, 1992

DEAR DIARY

I ran across the bridge today
To see Grandma and Granddad.

They cried with joy. They've lost weight
And aged since I last saw them

Four months ago. They told me
I had grown, that I was now a big girl,

Though I am only eleven. That's nature
For you. Children grow and

The elderly age. That's how it is
With those of us who are still alive.

SARAJEVO, SERBIA, SEPTEMBER 1992

PRECISELY

Offended by the Dutch peacekeeper
who had called him a Nazi, the Serb captain

said, "I understand his family's story,
OK, but I don't understand why

he's making such a fuss,"
abour the deportations.

"I understand why he gets emotional,
but they're not Jews, they're Muslims."

NEAR BRATUNAC, BOSNIA, JULY 1995

ON THE BUSES

On the buses as they drove past
I could see the women.

Pressing their faces to the windows,
eyes wide to stare at the men

lying in the grass by the road,
pools of blood under

their slashed necks. They all
forced themselves to look

in order to see if any of the men
were their husbands, fathers, and sons.

OUTSIDE SREBRENICA, SERBIA, 1995

MUSIC

The medic jabbed me with something
Then we both looked over the trench.
It was a seventeen-year-old girl soldier

Named Jacky, blonde ponytail, small Koran
On a leather strap around her neck. Some said
She was the commandant's mistress,

But in her tough voice she told them
She was there to fight. She was running with a box
Of ammunition beside a friend with short,

Spiked hair, carrying a Walkman
Playing hip-hop. During the shelling
They turned the music up.

NEAR KOSARE, KOSOVO, 12 MAY 1999

I TOLD THEM

"Look at me! You haven't killed all of us!"

SREBRENICA, 1999

LOOK, LOOK

He stood near the tent
On sentry duty, his helmet off,
An old Kalashnikov slung on his shoulder,
A cigarette in the corner of his mouth.

He was staring at the sky, bright blue
Flecked with pink and orange.
A perfect Turner landscape.
He was talking to himself,

Excited as a child. "Look, look
At the light," he said. "The beautiful light!"
Then he saw I was awake and
Turned to me with joy. "Look,

At the sky! We're still alive! Isn't it
Wonderful! We're still alive!"
I fell asleep again and when I woke up
Someone said he'd been sent to the front.

NEAR KOSARE, KOSOVO BORDER, MAY 1999

THE PLAN

He said, "You know, General,
We know how to deal with Albanian partisans."
I said, "Well, how do you do it?"

He said, "We've done this before."
I said, "When?"
He said, "Drenica, 1946."

I said, "How did you handle it?"
He said, "We killed all of them. It took
Several years, but we killed all of them."

BELGRADE, SERBIA, AUGUST 1999

FOR THE RECORD

Much later, when she met with the Dutch
Researcher, he seemed unaware
That children had been killed at Potočari.
"There were no children at Potočari,"
He said. She showed him
The photographs that proved there were.
"Well, then," she asked him, "did I kill my own children?
Did I do that to them?"
"There were no children," he repeated.
"No one knows where you women hid them."

THE HAGUE, THE NETHERLANDS, 2004

OK

"But please don't ask me
too much about that."

NEAR SREBRENICA, BOSNIA, 2004

BIT BY BIT

We felt it. It happened slowly.
But if you were smart
You could see it.

They started doing everything
Their own particular style,
Speaking and laughing a certain way.

On the bus, in the shops.
But before then,
We had all worked together,

Gone to school together.
Then we felt something
But we didn't believe it.

SREBRENICA, BOSNIA, 2005

EXILE

Seemingly infinite abundance...

JORDANIAN—SYRIAN BORDER, 2012

BE

Ruthless without anger
Aggressive without anger
Meeting violence with greater violence

Void of emotion
Not hindered by potential death

Be the loving father, spouse, and friend
As well as the ruthless killer

LOUISVILLE, KENTUCKY, 2013

SUGAR

I was so afraid I wanted to throw up.
I hugged my doll tight, saying "Don't be afraid,
don't be afraid, I'm here with you."

My parents gave us sugar, saying
it would help us be less afraid . . .
but I found it didn't change anything for me!

ALEPPO, SYRIA, 2013

WHAT ELSE?

You hear the siren or
Get a warning and then what?
We just wait there
Because there is no where to go.
What are we supposed to do,
Always be afraid?
Now we just pray.

NEAR THE TURKISH BORDER,
SYRIA, NOVEMBER 2015

JUST SO

I asked him if his soldiers had training
In how to treat civilians. "No,"
He replied, "to kill only, to save your life
and the life of your brother in arms.
You are an animal—a lizard
With a machine gun."

DEBALTSEVE, UKRAINE, 2014

GRAFFITI

Brother do not worry
the Belgian police have released me
for the 23rd time. Back to the lorry . . .
*
Remember put the tube in your mouth
and the other end out of the lorry's tarp cover
so you can breath
*
be careful that dog a lot
put oil on you & the dog cannot scent
*
Just look yourself and come yourself
as soon as possible. I am with Pichiu
there is much of control in the streets and
dangerous. If you have read this take the way
to Italy be careful what you doing
*
BE CAREFUL THEY DO NOT CATCH YOU
WITH DOGS IN THE PORT!!!
*
I am Sonu Kumar age 17
Brother don't worry moreover
I have possess a paper of Greece
*
Tomorrow we will try again—we will also . . .
*
I am Arash in Zeebrugge I have been sent back again
The one from the UK has deceive me
And also Belgium didn't mean anything
The human trafficker is Asad
*
Have try 12 times without success
Saw it too late left the assholes behind

PORT OF ZEEBRUGGE, BELGIUM, 2014

DECENCY

He had called his parents in a rush on August 8th.
"Mama, Papa I love you! Hi to everyone!
Kiss my daughter for me." His mother was told
Nine days later by an emissary of the Russian army
That her son Konstantin had died at the Ukranian border
In "army exercises." When she asked,
"Do you believe the words you are telling me?"
He had the decency to reply that he did not.

RUSSIAN—UKRANIAN BORDER, 13 AUGUST 2014

EPILOGUE

SOMEONE FROM PHARAE

He went to his room, where he kept the weapon
He'd used to kill the king
Conviction without morals made him cruel

But at the goat-footed theater
He covered his face and slipped away
Before the play was over, ashamed to be seen

Weeping for the women in an ancient story
Throughout the night
His eyes stayed open

The poet was wrong to say men without illusions
Are capable of any atrocity,
He thought

He cowered in his room
Like a bloodied cock dragged from the pit
By its spurs

DION, GREECE, 2ND CENTURY BCE

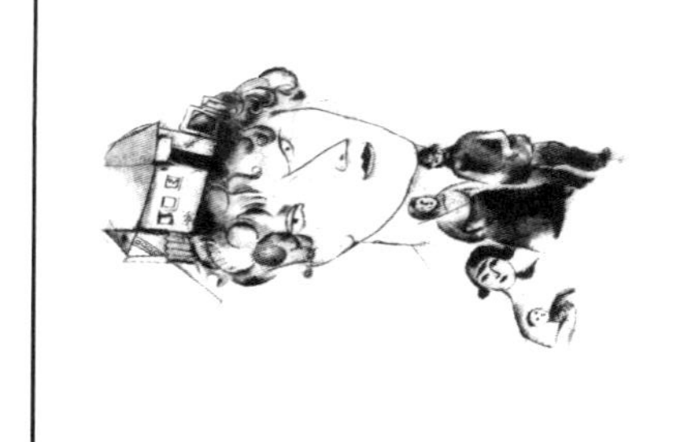

Chagall

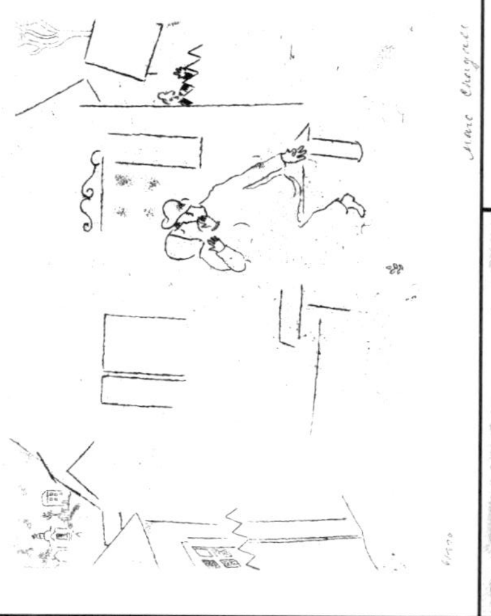

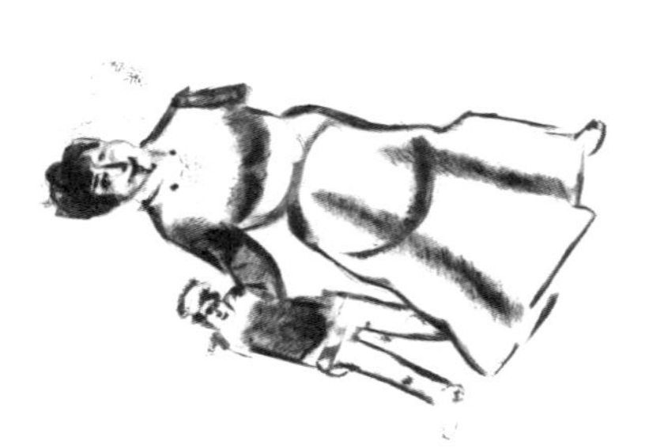

MARC

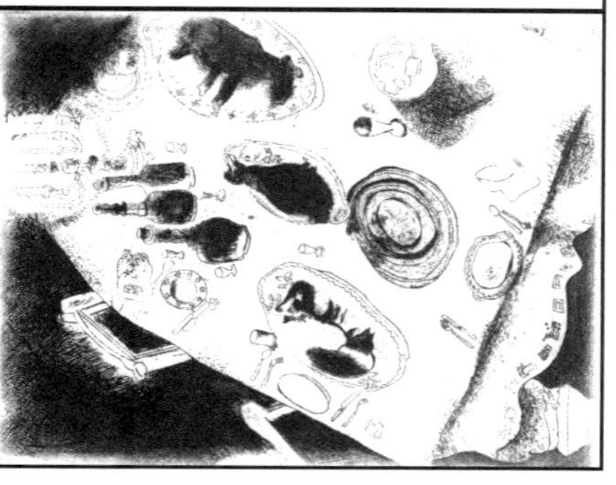

MARC CHAGALL ILLUSTRATIONS

from left to right

page ii

Chagall, Marc (1887–1985) ***The Eagle and the Beetle*** *(L'aigle et l'escarbot)*, 1927-1930. Etching from the unbound book *La Fontaine "Fables"* in two volumes containing 100 etchings by Marc Chagall to a text by La Fontaine. PLATE 38.9 x 30.1 CM. Publisher: Imprimerie Nationale de France. Rosenwald Collection National Gallery of Art, Washington, DC

page x

Chagall, Marc (1887–1985) © ARS, NY. ***Self Portrait*** *(Selbstportrait)* from *My Life (Mein Leben)*, 1922, published 1923. Etching and drypoint from a portfolio of twenty etchings (fifteen with drypoint). PLATE: 10⅞ x 8 9/16 IN (27.6 x 21.7 CM); SHEET: 17⅛ x 13⅛ IN (43.5 x 33.4 CM). Publisher: Paul Cassirer, Berlin. Printer: probably Pan-Presse, Berlin. Edition: 110. The Louis E. Stern Collection. The Museum of Modern Art, New York, NY, U.S.A. Digital Image © The Museum of Modern Art/Licensed by SCALA/ Art Resource, NY

page xii

Chagall, Marc (1887–1985) © ARS, NY. ***Lovers on the Bench*** *(Liebende auf der Bank)* from *My Life (Mein Leben)*, 1922, published 1923. Etching from a portfolio of twenty etchings (fifteen with drypoint). PLATE 5⅛ x 7 1/16 IN (13 x 18 CM); SHEET (IRREG.): 12⅝ x 16 5/16 IN (32 x 41.5 CM). Publisher: Paul Cassirer, Berlin. Printer: probably Pan-Presse, Berlin. Edition: 110. The Louis E. Stern Collection.The Museum of Modern Art, New York, NY, U.S.A. Digital Image © The Museum of Modern Art/Licensed by SCALA/ Art Resource, NY

page xiv

Chagall, Marc (1887–1985) © ARS, NY. **Man with Hen** *(L'Homme à la poule)*, 1922. Lithograph. COMPOSITION: 7 11/16 x 4 11/16 IN (19.6 x 11.9 CM); SHEET: 13⅞ x 10½ IN (35.2 x 26.6 CM). Edition: 35. Purchase. The Museum of Modern Art, New York, NY, U.S.A. Digital Image © The Museum of Modern Art/Licensed by SCALA / Art Resource,

NY. Image © The Museum of Modern Art/Licensed by SCALA/Art Resource, NY

page 22

Chagall, Marc (1887–1985) © ARS, NY. **The Table Piled with Food** *(La Table chargée de victuailles)*, PLATE XXXV (supplementary suite) from Les Âmes mortes, 1923-48. Etching and drypoint. PLATE 11 x 8⅝ IN (28 x 21.9 CM). The Louis E. Stern Collection. The Museum of Modern Art, New York, NY, U.S.A. Digital Image © The Museum of Modern Art/Licensed by SCALA/Art Resource, NY

page 48

Chagall, Marc (1887–1985) © ARS, NY. **Mutter und Sohn** *(Mother and Son)* from *My Life (Mein Leben)*, 1922, published 1923. Etching and drypoint from a portfolio of twenty etchings (fifteen with drypoint). PLATE 11 x 8 9/16 IN (28 x 21.8 CM); SHEET (IRREG.): 16 9/16 x 12⅝ IN (42 x 32.1 CM). Publisher: Paul Cassirer, Berlin. Printer: probably Pan-Presse, Berlin. Edition: 110. The Louis E. Stern Collection. The Museum of Modern Art, New York, NY, U.S.A. Digital Image © The Museum of Modern Art/Licensed by SCALA/Art Resource, NY

SOURCES

[P. V]

Etty Hillesum. *An Interrupted Life the Diaries, 1941-1943 and Letters from Westerbork.* Translated by Arnold J. Pomerans. NY: Picador, 1996.

Emanuele Artom. Diary entry addressed to his brother, Ennio. Excerpt translated by Siân Gibby,"The Diary of the Italian Resistance." Quoted in *Table Magazine,* November 30, 2017. https://www.tabletmag.com/sections/community/articles/diary-of-the-italian-resistance

Kazik (Simha Rotem). *Memoirs of a Warsaw Ghetto Fighter.* Translated by Barbara Harshav. New Haven: Yale University Press, 1994.

PART ONE [P. 1]

Conviction. Anon.

Night. The town crier of Ayvalik, as told by his son. The Greek Genocide Resource Center. http://www.greek-genocide.net

I Tell You. Mariam Baghdishian. Svazlian, Verjiné. *The Armenian Genocide: Testimonies and the Eyewitness Survivors.* Yerevan: Gitoutyoun Publishing House of NASRA (National Academy of Sciences, Armenia), 2011. Armenian Genocide Museum-Institute Foundation. http://www.genocid-museum.am/eng/aboutAGMI.php.

Mother. Mariam Baghdishian. Svazlian, *The Armenian Genocide.*

Wake Up. Mehmet Şükrü Saracoğlu. Akçam, Taner. *A Shameful Act: The Armenian Genocide and the Question of Turkish Responsibility.* Translated by Paul Bessemer. NY: Metropolitan, 2006, p. 362.

The Feast of Vardavar. Shogher Tonoyan. Svazlian, *The Armenian Genocide,* pp. 94-95.

At the Train Station. Akçam, *A Shameful Act,* p. 175.

An Open Field. Miller, Donald E. and Lorna Touryan Miller. *Survivors: An Oral History of the Armenian Genocide.* Berkeley: U of California Press, 1993, pp. 81-82.

That's Why. Miller and Miller, *Survivors*, pp. 86-88.

They Went to the City Hall. Henry Vartanian. Miller and Miller, *Survivors*, p. 146.

The Book. Hartunian, Abraham H. *Neither to Laugh nor to Weep: A Memoir of the Armenian Genocide.* Translated by Vartan Hartunian. Cambridge, MA: Armenian Heritage Press, 1986, p. 92.

Cucumbers. Hartunian, *Neither to Laugh*, p. 95.

Also. de Nogales, Rafael. *Four Years Beneath the Turkish Crescent.* NY: Scribner's, 1926.

Turkish Harem. The tattoo marks are a sign of their captivity and slavery. Vergeen Kalendarian (Virginia Meghrouni). Derdarian, Mae M. *Vergeen: A Survivor of the Armenian Genocide (Based on a Memoir by Virginia Meghrouni).* Los Angeles: Atmus, 1996, p. 65-66.

Who Knew? Vergeen Kalendarian (Virginia Meghrouni). Derdarian, *Vergeen*, p. 77.

Beauty, the Oldest Sorrow. Vergeen Kalendarian (Virginia Meghrouni). Derdarian, *Vergeen*, p. 48.

Deportees. Balakian, Grigorius. *Armenian Golgotha: A Memoir of the Armenian Genocide 1915–1918.* Translated by Peter Balakian with Aris Sevag. Vienna: Mekhitarist, 1922; NY: Random House, 2009, p. 200.

The Afterlife. Balakian, *Armenian Golgotha*, p. 146.

Who Would? Mkrtich Karapetian. Quoted in Svazlian, *The Armenian Genocide*, pp. 288-290.

Pigs. Mazhar Mufit, Hakkari deputy, addressing the Ankara National Assembly. Quoted in Akçam. *A Shameful Act*, p. 355.

Friendship. Kerr, Stanley E. *The Lions of Marash: Personal Experiences with American Near East Relief, 1919–1922.* Albany, NY: University of New York Press, 1973, p. 201.

And Forever. Gellhorn, Martha. *The Face of War.* London: Virago Press, 1986, pp. 37-38.

PART TWO [P. 23]

Like Gods. Germany occupied France in summer 1940. Infantryman Ernst Guicking. Quoted in Stargardt, Nicholas. *The German War: A Nation Under Arms, 1939–1945*. NY: Basic Books, 2015, p. 106.

Beautiful. From the diary of a Dutch woman who sympathized with the Nazis; her name was not disclosed by the holders of the diary, NIOD Institute for War, Holocaust and Genocide Studies in The Netherlands. Quoted in Nina Siegal and Josephine Sedgwick, "The Lost Diaries of War." *NY Times*, April 15, 2020. https://www.nytimes.com/interactive/2020/04/15/arts/dutch-war-diaries.html.

His Eyes. Ringelblum, Emmanuel. *Notes from the Warsaw Ghetto: The Journal of Emmanuel Ringelblum*. Translated by Jacob Sloan. NY: Schocken, 1974, p. 84.

Father. Wrobel, Etta. *From My Life My Way: The Extraordinary Memoir of a Jewish Partisan in WWII Poland*. Paradise Valley, PA: Wordsmithy, 2006. Quoted in The Jewish Partisan Educational Foundation http://www.jewishpartisans.org.

Today. Ringelblum, *Notes from the Warsaw Ghetto*.

Mother. Gutman, Israel. *Resistance: The Warsaw Ghetto Uprising*. NY: Houghton Mifflin, 1994, p. 139.

So. Reserve Policeman Hermann Gieschen. Quoted in Stargardt, *The German War*, p. 170.

Who Do We Thank? Anon.

Bridge of Ravens. Helm, Sarah. *Ravensbrück: Life and Death in Hitler's Concentration Camp for Women*. NY: Anchor, 2016, p. 211.

Obviously. Stargardt, *The German War*, p. 281.

Sunday Morning. Hillesum, *An Interrupted Life*, p. 145.

Sooner or Later. Anon.

A Journey. Helm, *Ravensbrück*, p. 270.

Hardly Any. Gen. George S. Patton. Quoted in Chaddick-Adams, Peter. *Snow and Steel: The Battle of the Bulge, 1944–45*. Oxford, UK: Oxford University Press, 2015, p. 79.

A Thin Ray of Brightness. Gefreiter Hans Hejny, 2nd Panzer Division. Quoted in Chaddick-Adams. *Snow and Steel*, p. 230.

More Light. Anon.

One Night. Klaudiusz Hrabyk. Quoted in Richie, Alexandra. *Warsaw 1944*. NY: FS&G, 2013, p. 428.

Escape. Lt. Hans Thieme, Wehrmacht 203rd Division. Quoted in Richie, *Warsaw 1944*, p. 370.

Goats. Anon.

Off the Coast, a Ship. After "Coral Island," a poem by Makiminato Tokuzo, translated by Katsunori Yamazato and Frank Stewart, in Yamazato, Katsunori and Frank Stewart, eds. *Living Spirit: Literature and Resurgence in Okinawa.* Honolulu: University of Hawai'i Press / *Mānoa*, 2011, pp. 180-181.

Abandoned. After "A Coral Island," a poem by Makiminato Tokuzo, translated by Katsunori Yamazato and Frank Stewart, in *Living Spirit*, pp. 180-181.

The Finest Thing. Großadmiral (Grand Admiral) Karl Doenitz. Quoted in Conot, Robert E. *Justice at Nuremberg.* NY: Harper & Row, 1983, p. 416.

Defiance. Sgt. Karel Čurda, Czech Nazi collaborator at his trial. Quoted in MacDonald, Callum. *The Killing of SS Obergrupenführer Reinharad Heydrich.* NY: The Free Press, 1989, p. 206.

The Sunflower. Wiesenthal, Simon. *The Sunflower.* Translated by H. A. Pichler et al. NY: Schocken, 1976, p. 96.

PART THREE [P. 49]

Pancakes. Leydesdorff, Selma. *Surviving the Bosnian Genocide: The Women of Srebrenica Speak.* Translated by Kay Richardson. Bloomington, IN: Indiana University Press, 2011, p. 99.

Foreigners. Drakulić, Slavanca. *The Balkan Express: Fragments from the Other Side of War.* NY: Norton, 1993, p. 56.

Dear Diary. Filipović, Zlata. *Zlata's Diary: A Child's Life in Sarajevo.* Translated by Christina Pribićhevich-Zorić. NY: Viking, 1994, p. 88.

Precisely. Rhoda, David. *Endgame: the Betrayal and Fall of Srebrenica, Europe's Worst Massacre since World War II.* NY: FS&G, 2012, p. 254.

On the Bus. Danner, *Stripping Bare the Body*, p. 286.

I Told Them. Jusufović, Jasmin Jusuf. "Remembering Srebrenica," http://www.srebrenica.org.uk/

Music. di Giovanni, Janine. *Madness Visible: A Memoir of War.* London: Bloomsbury, 2004, p. 5.

Look, Look. di Giovanni. *Madness Visible,* p. 33.

The Plan. Slobodan Milošević to General Wesley Clark, military head of NATO. Quoted in Judah, Tim. *Kosovo: War and Revenge.* New Haven: Yale University Press, 2000, p. 187.

OK. Timka Mujić. Quoted in Leydesdorff, *Surviving,* p. 15.

For the Record. Hasa Selmović. Quoted in Leydesdorff, *Survivors,* p. 19.

Bit by Bit. Vahida Ahmetovic. Quoted in Leydesdorff, *Survivors,* p. 65.

Exile. Anon.

Be. Bogel-Burroughs, "Kentucky Police Training Quoted Hitler and Urged 'Ruthless' Violence." *NY Times,* October 31, 2020.

Sugar. Myriam Rawick, age 9. Malterre, Thibauld. "Girl Chronicles Aleppo Terror in Myriam's Diary." *Business Insider,* 14 June 2017. https://www.businessinsider.com/afp-girl-chronicles-aleppo-terror-in-myriams-diary-2017-6.

Graffiti. From the walls of the Port of Zeebrugge police station. Derluyn, Ilse, Charles Watters, and Eric Broekaert. "'We are All the Same, Coz Exist Only One Earth, Why the BORDER EXIST': Messages of Migrants on their Way." *Journal of Refugee Studies,* 27:1 (2012).

What Else? Kafr Nbouda, resident of Jabal Harem IDP camp. Hall, Natsha. *Waiting for No One: Civilian Survival Strategies in Syria.* Washington, DC: Center for Civilians in Conflict, 2015, p. 19.

Just So. Ukranian soldier. Boneberger, Natliya. *"We Are Afraid of Silence": Protecting Civilians in the Donbass Region.* Washington, DC: Center for Civilians in Conflict, 2016, p. 38.

Decency. Konstantin Kuzmin. Quoted in Snyder, Timothy. *The Road to Unfreedom: Russia, Europe, America.* NY: Tim Dugan Books, 2018, p. 189.

EPILOGUE [P. 67]

Someone from Pharae. Anon.

SELECTED READINGS

BOOKS

Akçam, Taner. *A Shameful Act: The Armenian Genocide and the Question of Turkish Responsibility*. Translated by Paul Bessemer. NY: Metropolitan, 2006.

Applebaum, Anne. *Gulag: A History*. NY: Anchor Books, 2004.

Babcock, Robert O. *War Stories: Volume I: D-Day to the Liberation of Paris*. Athens, GA: Deeds, 2014.

Balakian, Grigorius. *Armenian Golgotha: A Memoir of the Armenian Genocide 1915–1918*. Translated by Peter Balakian with Aris Sevag. Vienna: Mekhitarist, 1922; NY: Random House, 2009.

Balakian, Peter. *The Burning Tigris: The Armenian Genocide and America's Response*. NY: Harper Collins, 2003.

Boneberger, Natliya. *"We Are Afraid of Silence": Protecting Civilians in the Donbass Region*. Washington, DC: Center for Civilians in Conflict, 2016.

Chaddick-Adams, Peter. *Snow and Steel: The Battle of the Bulge, 1944–45*. Oxford, UK: Oxford University Press, 2015.

Conot, Robert E. *Justice at Nuremberg*. NY: Harper & Row, 1983.

Danner, Mark. *Stripping Bare the Body: Politics Violence War*. NY: Nation Books, 2009.

Davies, Norman. *Rising '44: The Battle for Warsaw*. NY: Viking, 2005.

de Jong, Louis. *The Netherlands and Nazi Germany*. Cambridge, MA: Harvard University Press, 1990.

de Nogales, Rafael. *Four Years Beneath the Turkish Crescent*. Translated by Muna Lee. London: Scribner's, 1926.

Derdarian, Mae M. *Vergeen: A Survivor of the Armenian Genocide (Based on a Memoir by Virginia Meghrouni)*. Los Angeles: Atmus, 1996.

di Giovanni, Janine. *Madness Visible: A Memoir of War*. London: Bloomsbury, 2004.

________________. *The Morning They Came for Us: Dispatches from Syria.* NY: Liveright, 2017.

Drakulić, Slavenka. *The Balkan Express: Fragments from the Other Side of War.* NY: Norton, 1993.

Elkins, Caroline. *Imperial Reckoning: The Untold Story of Britain's Gulag in Kenya.* NY: Holt, 2005.

Elliott, Mabel Everlyn. *Beginning Again at Ararat.* NY: Revelle, 1924.

Filipović, Zlata. *Zlata's Diary: A Child's Life in Sarajevo.* Translated by Christina Pribićhevich-Zorić. NY: Viking, 1994.

Gellhorn, Martha. *The Face of War.* London: Virago Press, 1986.

Grossman, Vasily. *A Writer at War: A Soviet Journalist with the Red Army, 1941-1945.* NY: Vintage, 2007.

Gutman, Israel. *Resistance: The Warsaw Ghetto Uprising.* NY: Houghton Mifflin, 1994.

Halili, Qëndresë. *War Diary: We Children of Kosovo, We Children of the War.* Bloomington, IN: AuthorHouse, 2017.

Hall, Natsha. *Waiting for No One: Civilian Survival Strategies in Syria.* Washington, DC: Center for Civilians in Conflict, 2015.

Hartunian, Abraham H. *Neither to Laugh nor to Weep: A Memoir of the Armenian Genocide.* Translated by Vartan Hartunian. Cambridge, MA: Armenian Heritage Press, 1986.

Hillesum, Etty. *An Interrupted Life the Diaries, 1941–1943 and Letters from Westerbork.* Translated by Arnold J. Pomerans. NY: Picador, 1996.

Helm, Sarah. *Ravensbrück: Life and Death in Hitler's Concentration Camp for Women.* NY: Anchor, 2016.

Hochschild, Adam. *To End All Wars: A Story of Loyalty and Rebellion, 1914–1918.* NY: Houghton Mifflin Harcourt, 2011.

Judah, Tim. *Kosovo: War and Revenge.* New Haven: Yale University Press, 2000.

Kazik (Simha Rotem). *Memoirs of a Warsaw Ghetto Fighter.* Translated by Barbara Harshav. New Haven: Yale University Press, 1994.

Yamazato, Katsunori and Frank Stewart, eds. *Living Spirit: Literature and Resurgence in Okinawa.* Honolulu: University of Hawai'i Press / *Mānoa*, 2011.

Kelly, Aisling C. "Refugee Mother's Experiences of Forced Migration and Its Impact upon Family Life." Thesis submitted to the University of Hertfordshire in partial fulfillment of the requirements of the degree of Doctor of Clinical Psychology. April 2015. Unpublished.

Kerr, Stanley E. *The Lions of Marash: Personal Experiences with American Near East Relief, 1919–1922*. Albany, NY: University of New York Press, 1973.

Leydesdorff, Selma. *Surviving the Bosnian Genocide: The Women of Srebrenica Speak*. Translated by Kay Richardson. Bloomington, IN: Indiana University Press, 2011.

Maas, Peter. *Love Thy Neighbor: A Story of War*. NY: Knopf, 1996.

McAllester, Mathew. *Beyond the Mountains of the Damned: The War Inside Kosovo*. NY: New York University Press, 2003.

MacDonald, Callum. *The Killing of SS Obergrupenführer Reinharad Heydrich*. NY: The Free Press, 1989.

Mazower, Mark. *Inside Hitler's Greece: The Experience of Occupation, 1941–44*. New Haven: Yale University Press, 1993.

Mechanicus, Philip. *Waiting for Death: A Diary*. Translated by Susan Ridder. London: Calder and Boyars, 1968.

Miller, Donald E. and Lorna Touryan Miller. *Survivors: An Oral History of the Armenian Genocide*. Berkeley: University of California Press, 1993.

Morgenthau, Henry. *Ambassador Morgenthau's Story*. Detroit: Wayne State University Press, 2003.

Prior, Robin. *Gallipoli: The End of the Myth*. New Haven: Yale University Press, 2009.

Psychoundakis, George. *The Cretan Runner*. Translated by Patrick Leigh Fermor. London: John Murray, 1955.

Purdom, C. B. (ed.). *Everyman at War: Sixty Personal Narratives of the War*. London: Dent, 1930.

Richie, Alexandra. *Warsaw 1944*. NY: FS&G, 2013.

Ringelblum, Emmanuel. *Notes from the Warsaw Ghetto: The Journal of Emmanuel Ringelblum*. Translated by Jacob Sloan. NY: Schocken, 1974.

Rhoda, David. *Endgame: the Betrayal and Fall of Srebrenica, Europe's Worst Massacre since World War II.* NY: FS&G, 2012.

Snyder, Timothy. *The Road to Unfreedom: Russia, Europe, America.* NY: Tim Dugan Books, 2018.

Stargardt, Nicholas. *The German War: A Nation Under Arms, 1939–1945.* NY: Basic Books, 2015.

Sudetic, Chuck. *Blood and Vengeance: One Family's Story of the War in Bosnia.* NY: Norton, 1998.

Suny, Ronald G. *Looking Toward Ararat: Armenia in Modern History.* Bloomington, IN: Indiana University Press, 1993.

Svazlian, Verjiné. *The Armenian Genocide: Testimonies and the Eyewitness Survivors.* Yerevan: Gitoutyoun Publishing House of NASRA (National Academy of Sciences, Armenia), 2011.

Wiesenthal, Simon. *The Sunflower.* Translated by H. A. Pichler et al. NY: Schocken, 1976.

ARTICLES

Bogel-Burroughs, Nicholas. "Kentucky Police Training Quoted Hitler and Urged 'Ruthless' Violence." *NY Times,* October 31, 2020.

Derluyn, Ilse, Charles Watters, and Eric Broekaert. "'We are All the Same, Coz Exist Only One Earth, Why the BORDER EXIST': Messages of Migrants on their Way." *Journal of Refugee Studies,* 27:1 (2012).

Gibby, Siân. "The Diary of the Italian Resistance." *Table Magazine,* November 30, 2017. https://www. tabletmag.com/sections/community/articles/diary-of-the-italian-resistance

Kirillova, Kseniya. "War Through a Child's Eyes: 9-Year-Old's Diary about Kosovo War Now in English." *Euromaidan Press: News and Views from Ukraine.* 2017/07/25. http://euromaidanpress.com/2017/07/25/kosovo-diary/

Malterre, Thibauld. "Girl Chronicles Aleppo Terror in Myriam's Diary." *Business Insider,* 14 June 2017. https://www.businessinsider.com/afp-girl-chronicles-aleppo-terror-in-myriams-diary-2017-6.

Siegal, Nina and Josephine Sedgwick. "The Lost Diaries of War." *NY Times,* April 15, 2020: https://www.nytimes.com/interactive/2020/04/15/arts/dutch-war-diaries.html

ONLINE

ARCHIVE.ORG
archive.org

ARCHIVES OF THE UNITED STATES
archives.gov/research/guide-fed-records/groups/165.html

ARMENIAN GENOCIDE MUSEUM—INSTITUTE FOUNDATION
genocid-museum.am/eng

EUROMAIDAN PRESS
euromaidanpress.com/2017/07/25/kosovo-diary

FIRSTWORLDWAR.COM
firstworldwar.com

GREEK GENOCIDE RESOURCE CENTER
greek-genocide.net

HISTORYNET. COM
historynet.com/i-will-fight-to-the-last-wwii-japanese-soldier-diary-june-1943.htm

JEWISH PARTISAN EDUCATIONAL FOUNDATION
jewishpartisans.org

LIBRARY OF CONGRESS VETERANS HISTORY PROJECT
loc.gov/vets/stories/wwiilist.html

MUSEUMS VICTORIA MILITARY MEMORABILIA COLLECTION
museumsvictoria.com.au/ask-us/wwi-australian-military-history

NIOD INSTITUTE FOR WAR, HOLOCAUST AND GENOCIDE STUDIES
niod.nl

SREBRENICA.COM
srebrenica.org.uk

UNITED STATES HOLOCAUST MEMORIAL MUSEUM
ushmm.org

ABOUT THE AUTHOR

FRANK STEWART is the author of four previous books of poetry and a book of non-fiction, and has edited numerous anthologies of poetry, essays, and fiction. He received the Whiting Writers Award and the Hawai'i Governors Award for Literature, among other honors. He lives in Honolulu and edits *Mānoa: A Pacific Journal of International Writing.*